SCHOLASTIC

Teaching Reading With Donald Crews Books

BY PAMELA CHANKO

NEW YORK • TORONTO • LONDON • AUCKLAND • SYDNEY

MEXICO CITY • NEW DELHI • HONG KONG • BUENOS AIRES

Teaching *Resources*

For Daniel and Ariel,

who are on the right track

and will travel far.

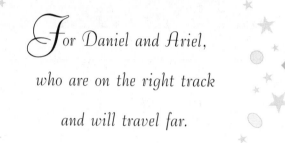

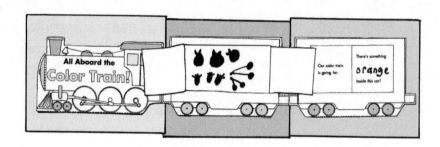

ACKNOWLEDGMENTS

*Special thanks to Kama Einhorn and the Scholastic team for always keeping me
in the loop and up to speed!*

Cover from *Freight Train* by Donald Crews. Used by permission of HarperCollins Publishers. Copyright © 1978 by Donald Crews.

Cover from *School Bus* by Donald Crews. Used by permission of HarperCollins Publishers. Copyright © 1984 by Donald Crews.

Cover from *Ten Black Dots* by Donald Crews. Used by permission of HarperCollins Publishers. Copyright © 1968 by Donald Crews.

Cover and interior design by Kathy Massaro
Interior art by Maxie Chambliss, except for page 57 by James Graham Hale

ISBN-13: 978-0-439-63522-6
ISBN-10: 0-439-63522-5
Copyright © 2008 by Pamela Chanko
Published by Scholastic Inc.
All rights reserved.
Printed in the U.S.A.

2 3 4 5 6 7 8 9 10   40   15 14 13 12 11 10 09 08

Contents

About This Book

*T*hrough spare, simple text and bold, graphic artwork, author-illustrator Donald Crews creates innovative books that celebrate the exciting motion of everyday life. The story lines are often simple: a truck is loaded with cargo, starts on its journey, and arrives at its destination. A carousel takes on riders, begins spinning, and slows to a stop. By presenting high-interest subjects with surprising simplicity, Crews allows the central concepts to shine through with a clarity that is as educational as it is engaging. His books provide a perfect venue for children to discover, explore, and interpret the objects and actions that make up their environment.

The lessons and activities in this book will help children deepen their understanding of the concepts and themes presented in Crews's work. They also support learning across the curriculum, with a focus on helping children master essential reading skills. In addition to a description and summary of each book, here's a look at what you'll find in each lesson:

◎ **Concepts and Themes:** See at a glance the central concepts and themes presented in the book.

◎ **Before Reading:** These suggestions and activities tap prior knowledge and prepare children for the literature experience by inviting them to make predictions, ask questions, make connections, build vocabulary, and more.

◎ **After Reading:** Discussion ideas and questions that focus on predictable text and picture clues help children develop strategies for making sense of text. Ideas for exploring setting and plot, and practice in sequencing and retelling, also support comprehension. Sample questions to guide children's thinking help them make inferences and relate what they read to their own experiences. Fresh and creative activities—many with interactive reproducibles—extend children's learning across the curriculum.

◎ **Word Play:** These mini-lessons focus on elements of language including word choice, text features, and poetic devices (such as onomatopoeia).

Whether you choose to explore the author's work as a whole, or simply dip into his books from time to time throughout the year, this book will provide you with a wealth of ideas for keeping children's learning right on track. So climb aboard and take children on an exciting journey with Donald Crews!

Assessment Ideas

During a thematic unit, it's important to use several different assessments, depending on the children and the activity or project they are involved with. A couple of suggestions follow:

◎ **Rubrics and Checklists of Desired Behaviors:** Rubrics and checklists, including self-assessments, make it easy to document children's project work. Repeating a rubric over the course of a thematic unit or project provides a record of growth.

◎ **Sticky-Note Assessment Folders:** Place a sticky note for each child in a folder. Use the sticky notes to jot down anecdotal records related to assessment. This makes it convenient to gather assessment information while observing and working with children. Transfer the notes to children's individual folders for a record of their work during a lesson, activity, or project.

Name _____ Date _____

Assessment Checklist

Skills	Skill Mastered	Skill at Emergent Level	Skill Not Yet Demonstrated
Asks questions while reading.			
Uses pictures in the book as sequencing clues.			
Uses vocabulary for time order.			
Provides details that support main idea.			

Connections to the Language Arts Standards

The activities in this book are designed to support the following standards outlined by Mid-continent Research for Education and Learning (McREL), an organization that collects and synthesizes national and state K–12 curriculum standards.

Uses the general skills and strategies of the reading process:

◆ Understands how print is organized and read

◆ Creates mental images from pictures and print

◆ Uses meaning clues to aid comprehension and make predictions about content

Uses reading skills and strategies to understand and interpret a variety of literary texts:

◆ Understands a variety of familiar texts, both fiction and nonfiction

◆ Knows main ideas or theme, setting, main characters, main events, sequence, and problems in stories

◆ Makes simple inferences regarding the order of events and possible outcomes

◆ Relates stories to personal experiences

Uses the general skills and strategies of the writing process:

◆ Uses writing and other methods to describe familiar persons, places, objects, or experiences

◆ Writes in a variety of forms or genres, including responses to literature

Kendall, J. S. & Marzano, R. J. (2004). *Content knowledge: A compendium of standards and benchmarks for K–12 education.* Aurora, CO: Mid-continent Research for Education and Learning. Online database: http://www.mcrel.org/standards-benchmarks/

Meet Donald Crews

Donald Crews was born on August 30, 1938, in Newark, New Jersey. His mother worked as a seamstress, and also designed and made her own clothing. His father worked for the railroad. Both parents contributed to their child's development as an author and artist: his mother's eye for design and his father's work in the transportation industry are both evident factors in the books Donald Crews grew up to create. His grandparents also played an important role. Each summer, Donald traveled on a train with his mother, brother, and sisters to stay at his grandparents' farm in Cottondale, Florida. He spent many hours on the front porch of the farmhouse, watching the trains go by. The movement of those trains would later provide a source of inspiration for some of the author-illustrator's most celebrated works.

Young Donald was a good student at school and was noticed for his artistic talent. In high school, he was encouraged by one of his teachers to pursue a career as an artist. Crews went on to study at Cooper Union for the Advancement of Science and Art in New York City, from which he graduated in 1959. He married another Cooper Union graduate, Ann Jonas, and the couple went to work as graphic artists. It was this work that led to Crews's career as a children's author and illustrator. One of the pieces he created for his portfolio was an innovative alphabet book. When it was suggested that the piece might make a good children's book, Crews submitted it to publishers—and *We Read: A to Z* was published in 1967.

Crews went on to meet with great success as a children's author and artist, using his own experiences to inspire his work. Drawing from his early fascination with trains, Crews created *Freight Train*, which was named a 1979 Caldecott Honor Book. *Truck* (another Caldecott Honor Book) was also inspired by real-life experiences. Crews grew up near a commercial truck depot and loved to watch the brightly colored trucks come and go. Crews works from images that interest him: "I took pictures of bicycle races for years," he said, "never thinking they'd be the subject of a book. But, eventually, those photos led to *Bicycle Race*." In fact, all of Crews's subjects are drawn from real life: the excitement of a city parade, a flight on an airplane, a ride on a carousel, and, of course, the author's own childhood summers in Cottondale.

Donald Crews has a talent for expressing the interest, excitement, and wonder inherent in everyday objects and experiences. Perhaps this is what makes his books so appealing to young children—they, too, are experiencing and discovering the world with a fresh eye. When asked what he wants readers to take away from his books, Crews replied: "I think just of an adventure, an involvement with observation, a learning to look, to be more observant about what you see." And Donald Crews helps us see our world in a truly unique way.

Donald Crews photo courtesy of Nina Crews.

Activities to Use With Any Donald Crews Book

As children become familiar with Donald Crews's work, they will see that many of his books are tied together by the theme of transportation and movement. In addition to the activities suggested for each featured title, you can use the following ideas to help children make connections between concepts in the books and explore the theme of transportation as a whole.

Vehicle Watch

What kinds of vehicles do people use most often to get around your neighborhood? Do a "vehicle watch" to find out.

1. Create a record sheet by drawing three or four vehicles down the left side of a sheet of paper (such as a car, bus, truck, and bicycle) and make a copy for each child.

2. Distribute the sheets to small groups of children and take them to an area where they can safely observe traffic. Set a time limit for your vehicle watch (such as five or ten minutes). Then have children track the vehicles that go past by making a tally mark in the appropriate row for each vehicle they see. Depending on how much traffic there is in your area, you might choose to assign each child in the group a different vehicle to watch for.

3. Take different groups of children on a watch each day for a week. At the end of the week, help groups tally the results. What conclusions can children make about how people travel in your neighborhood? Ask questions, such as:

   - Do most people drive their own vehicles, or take public transportation?

   - How many people ride bicycles?

   - Do more trucks or buses travel in this area?

   Help children connect their findings with the type of community you live in: for instance, if you live in a rural area in which destinations are spread out across long distances, children may not see many bicycle riders. If you live in a city with a large population, more people may take buses to get from place to place.

Teaching Tip

To add illustrations, you can use the vehicle patterns on page 10, if desired.

◆ To create the frieze at
one time, give each
child one or more sheets
(depending on the
number of children in
your class) and help
children research
vehicles or other
transportation-related
words that begin with
their letter.

◆ To build your display
gradually, leave the
sheets in a central
location and encourage
children to fill them out
as they find words that
begin with each letter.

Alphabet on the Move

There are so many kinds of things that go—can children find a
transportation word for each letter of the alphabet?

1. As children learn about different types of transportation, work together
to build an alphabet frieze for your classroom. Build the frieze all at once
(by assigning each child a different letter) or build it gradually as you
encounter new forms of transportation and related vocabulary words.
(See Teaching Tips, left.) To begin, prepare 26 sheets of construction
paper, labeling each one with an uppercase and lowercase letter.

2. Invite children to a draw a picture on each sheet and write or dictate a
label (for instance, *Aa–Ambulance, Bb–Bicycle, Cc–Car, Dd–Dump
truck, Ee–Engine*). Encourage children to be creative for the more
challenging letters. For example, *X* might be for *X-press Train* or
Railroad X-ing, *Q* might be for *Quick-moving racecar*, and *Z* might be
for *Zeppelin*.

3. Post the completed sheets in alphabetical order across a wall of the
classroom. Children will look at their ABC's in a whole new way!

Transport Sort

Teaching Tip

▲▲▲▲▲▲

Encourage children to state
their sorting criteria before
they begin and explain
their reasoning as they sort.

Children observe and classify to group vehicles by different attributes.

1. Collect a variety of toy vehicles for sorting activities, including cars,
trucks, planes, trains, buses, and boats. If possible, include vehicles
with different functions, such as a fire truck, police car, tugboat, school
bus, and so on.

2. To begin, ask children to sort the vehicles by color or shape. As they
learn more about each vehicle, encourage them to come up with more
challenging sorting categories, such as number of wheels, modes of
travel (air, land, and water), or how the vehicle is used (to carry people
or cargo, for emergencies or recreation, and so on).

On-the-Go Bingo

Reinforce the names of different vehicles and how they travel with the game on pages 10–11. The game can be played with two players.

1. Make copies of the cards and game boards and cut them apart along the dotted lines only. Give each player one game board and a supply of Bingo markers (such as math unit cubes or dried beans). Place the cards in a paper bag.

2. To play, reach into the bag and pick a card. Read the name of the vehicle and show the picture to children. Players who have the same vehicle on their game board should put a marker over each space on which it appears.

3. Continue until a player has a line of four markers in a row (vertical, horizontal, or diagonal) and that child calls out "On-the-Go Bingo!" Then play the game again.

Variation: As an added challenge, talk with children about where each vehicle travels—on land, on water, or through the air. They will notice that six types of each vehicle are represented in the game. Then invite children to play a new version:

◎ Rather than trying to cover any four vehicles in a row, the object of this game is to cover every space on the board that shows one classification of vehicle: air, land, or water. For instance, a player's board might have a helicopter, airplane, balloon, blimp, and rocket. If all those spaces are covered (and there are no other aircraft on the board), the player can call out "Air Bingo!" The same rules apply for calling "Land Bingo!" or "Water Bingo!"

On-the-Go Bingo Cards

car

airplane

rowboat

truck

helicopter

sailboat

bus

blimp

liner

bicycle

glider

steamboat

van

balloon

tugboat

train

rocket

canoe

Teaching Reading With Donald Crews Books © 2008 by Pamela Chanko, Scholastic Teaching Resources

On-the-Go Bingo

On-the-Go Bingo

Teaching Reading With Donald Crews Books © 2008 by Pamela Chanko, Scholastic Teaching Resources

11

School Bus

◆

(GREENWILLOW, 1984)

Concepts and Themes

▲▲▲▲▲▲

☼ vehicles:
school buses

☼ transportation:
home to school

☼ opposites:
empty/full, stop/go,
large/small

Through bold illustrations and simple text, this book follows the school bus as it travels around town during a single day's work. Large or small, these buses have one job to do: to take children to school and bring them home again. But where do the buses go when the children have all gone home? The buses go home, too, of course—to a parking lot, where they wait for the next day's journey to begin.

Before Reading

Activate children's prior knowledge about school buses. Do any children take a bus to school each day? Encourage children to share their experiences by asking:

✳ Where does the bus pick you up? Who waits for the bus with you?

✳ Does the bus make a lot of stops on the way to school? What happens at each stop?

✳ Where does the bus drop you off when school is over? Where do you think it goes next?

Invite children who do not travel on the school bus to share their experiences with other kinds of buses. Ask:

✳ Have you ever ridden on a bus? Where were you going? Was it a long trip or a short one?

✳ Did the bus make any stops on the way? How did the bus driver know when to stop?

After Reading

Talk with children about the job a school bus does each day. Can children retell the sequence of events in the book? Ask:

✳ When the school bus starts on its trip each morning, is it empty or full? What happens next?

✳ What do the school buses do while children are at school? After the children have gone home? Were you surprised to see that the school bus has a "home" as well?

✳ What traffic signs did you notice in the book? How do these signs help the bus driver? How do they help keep people safe?

This Is the Way We Go to School Math & Social Studies

Reinforce graphing skills with a transportation chart that shows how children get to school each day.

1. Survey children to find out how they travel to school. Create a graph on a large sheet of tagboard. Label it with column headings such as "Bus," "Car," "Bicycle," "Train," and "Walk." (You might also add drawings or use copies of the vehicles on page 10.) Provide children with index cards labeled with their names. Children can also draw a small picture of themselves on the card.

2. Invite children up to the graph and have them use a bubble of removable tape to attach their card under the method of transportation they use most often to get to school. When the graph is complete, discuss the results by asking questions, such as:

   * How do most of the children in our class get to school?
   * How do the fewest children get to school?
   * How many children walk to school? Take the school bus?
   * Do more children take the bus or ride in a car?

You might also discuss where children live in relation to school. How does the distance affect the method of transportation they use?

How We Get to School				
Bus	Car	Bicycle	Train	Walk

Who Drives the Bus? Writing & Social Studies

What is it like to drive a school bus? Find out by going to the source! If possible, invite one of the bus drivers for your school (or a neighboring school) to visit your classroom for an interview. (If a personal visit is not possible, you might help children do research about the job using library books or the Internet.) In a shared writing activity, help children prepare for the interview by brainstorming a list of questions for the driver. Topics of interest might include:

◎ How did you learn to drive a school bus? Is it different from driving a car?

◎ How many stops do you make each day?

(*continues*)

Word Play

* Use the opposite word pairs in *School Bus* to begin a word wall. First, help children find these opposite word pairs in the book: *large/small, stop/go, empty/full.* Then help children think of more opposites by naming a word and inviting them to supply its opposite (for instance, *up/down, near/far, short/tall*). Write each word pair on a large index card. Post all the cards on a bulletin board and have children use them to write a story or poem full of opposites.

* To turn your word wall into a challenging puzzle, puzzle-cut each index card in two to separate the words. Then mix up all the pieces. Invite children to fit the pieces back together, matching each word with its opposite.

@ What do you do when children are at school? Where do you take the bus after children go home?

@ Why are school buses yellow?

@ What rules do you have to follow when you drive the bus?

Encourage your visitor to talk with children about important safety rules they should follow while riding the bus and when getting on and off. After the interview, you might have children create pictures showing what they learned and present them to the bus driver as a thank-you.

Sign Scavenger Hunt Reading & Social Studies

There are many important traffic signs included in the illustrations for *School Bus*. How many of these signs can you find in your neighborhood?

@ Look through the book with children to find examples of traffic signs. Some they will notice are *Walk*, *Don't Walk*, *Stop*, and *School*. Then take a walk around the neighborhood to find examples of each sign. Where are the signs located? What do they tell people to do? Encourage children to look for additional signs as well, such as *One Way*, *Do Not Enter*, and *Yield*.

@ Back in the classroom, invite children to create their own versions of the signs on construction paper or tagboard. For a fun extension, you might post the signs around the classroom to create a "traffic route." Children can pretend to be school bus drivers and follow the signs to get from one end of the classroom to the other.

The Wheels on the Bus Music & Movement

Invite children to show what they've learned about school buses by creating their own words for a well-known song. Begin by singing the traditional version of *The Wheels on the Bus*:

> The wheels on the bus go round and round,
> Round and round, round and round,
> The wheels on the bus go round and round,
> All around the town.

Next, invite children to use their knowledge about school buses to create new lyrics, for instance, *the children on the bus get on and off, the driver of the bus makes lots of stops*, and *the signs on the street say "stop" and "go."* You can turn this into a movement activity by inviting children to role-play bus drivers and passengers. Encourage them to act out their school bus journey as they sing.

Who's on the Bus?

Art & Social Studies

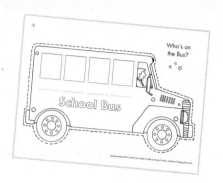

Use the reproducible on page 16 to create a lift-the-flap school bus display.

1. Make one copy of the reproducible for each child. Distribute the school bus patterns and help children cut them out.

2. Assist children in cutting along three sides of each window, as shown, to create flaps. Have children glue the bus to a sheet of construction paper, making sure they do not glue down the flaps. Children can decorate their buses with crayons or markers. Then have them fold back the flaps to create open windows.

3. Invite children to draw passengers in the windows, such as pictures of themselves and their classmates. They might also enjoy creating "theme buses" of favorite story characters or animals. Have children write or dictate the name of each passenger on the line beneath each window.

4. When children have finished, fold the flaps back down and display the buses on a wall of the classroom. Children can take turns reading the passengers' names on each bus and then lifting the flaps to see who's inside!

Book Links

Bus Stop, Bus Go!
by Daniel Kirk
(Putnam, 2001).

Invite children along on a hectic school bus ride with Tommy—and his escaped pet hamster!

Maisy Drives the Bus
by Lucy Cousins
(Candlewick, 2000).

Ride along with the beloved mouse as she picks up a new animal friend at each bus stop.

This Is the Way We Go to School
by Edith Baer
(Scholastic, 1990).

Through rhyming text, this book shows the many methods of transportation used by children all over the world to get to school each day.

The Wheels on the Bus
by Maryann Kovalski
(Little Brown & Co., 1987).

When two girls and their grandma decide to pass the time by singing as they wait for the bus, they get so carried away that they miss the bus altogether. Taxi!

Who's on the Bus?

School Bus

Truck

⬩⬩⬩

(G R E E N W I L L O W ,   1 9 8 0)

The bold illustrations of *Truck* earned this book a Caldecott Honor. Wordless except for the signs on the road and on the vehicles, the story's pictures show the journey of a truck—from loading the cargo, to traveling through city streets, to zooming along superhighways, to stopping at an all-night diner. As the journey comes to an end, the cargo is unloaded—and a truck-full of tricycles is delivered.

Before Reading

Invite children to tell what they know about trucks. Ask:

* What are some different kinds of trucks, and what do they do? What is a fire truck for? How about a dump truck?

* Have you ever seen trucks traveling through your neighborhood? What did they look like? Where do you think they were going?

* Have you ever seen a truck making a delivery, such as a food truck parked outside a supermarket? What are some other things a truck might deliver?

* How is a truck different from a car?

Show children the cover of the book and invite them to make predictions about the story. Ask:

* Where do you think this truck is going? What do you think will happen when it gets there?

After Reading

After sharing the book once with children, page through it again, inviting them to narrate the truck's journey. Guide children's narrations with questions, such as:

* What is the truck carrying? Where do you think the tricycles need to go?

* What other kinds of vehicles are on the road with the truck? What might some of the other trucks on the highway be carrying?

* Why do you think the truck stopped at the diner? Do you think it would be hard to be a truck driver and travel such a long distance?

* What does the truck need to help keep it going? What do you think the pump next to the diner was for?

* Did you recognize any of the street or highway signs? What do they tell drivers to do? How do they help keep people safe on the road?

Concepts and Themes

▲▲▲▲▲▲

☼ vehicles: trucks

☼ highways, driving

☼ shipping, deliveries

☼ long-distance travel

Word ·°· Play

Page through the book, stopping to point out the words *trucking* and *moving*. Write both words on the board and ask: "What do these two words have in common?" (*They both end with* ing.) Can children think of any other words that end in *ing*? Make a list together (*walking, flying, playing, diving*). Then review your list and underline each base word. Point out that words that end with *e* (such as *move* and *dive*) require a spelling change. Children should drop the *e* before adding *ing*.

Create Captions Writing

Although *Truck* is a wordless book, it tells the story of an exciting trip. Invite children to create their own captions describing the truck's journey.

1. Page through the book with children, inviting them to point to any print they see. Ask: "Where is the print on the page?" (*On the trucks and on the road signs.*) "Are there any words that tell a story?" (*No.*) Explain that in this book, the author chose to let the pictures tell the story—but children can add their own words to create a written one.

2. Gather several large sticky notes and take children through the book page by page. Encourage them to use the illustrations and their knowledge of story structure as a guide to create a caption for each page. For instance, the first few pages might read: *The big red truck was loaded up with tricycles. Then it started on its trip. There were many street signs for the driver to follow.* As children dictate captions, write them on the sticky notes and attach them to the bottom of each page. When the story is complete, read your new story aloud to the group.

Truck Chart Writing & Social Studies

Help children learn about different kinds of trucks and the many jobs they do.

1. Provide children with magazines and catalogs that contain pictures of different kinds of trucks, including fire trucks, dump trucks, flatbed trucks, cement mixers, and so on. (Catalogs from car and truck dealerships are a good resource.) Invite children to cut out the trucks they find.

2. Create a three-column chart on a large sheet of tagboard. Place the truck pictures in the first column, and write the name of the truck in the second column. Then help children research how each truck is used, and write a short description of its use in the third column. For instance, a milk truck carries milk from the farm to the factory; a moving truck helps people move their belongings to a new home; and a tow truck helps cars that are in trouble on the road. Continue to add to your chart as children find pictures and learn truck facts.

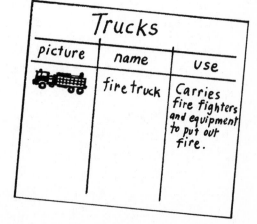

Trucks		
picture	name	use
🚒	fire truck	Carries fire fighters and equipment to put out fire.

Truck Mini-Book Reading: Sequencing

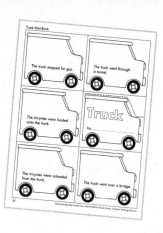

Help children retell the story's sequence with a truck-shaped mini-book.

1. Make one copy of the reproducible on page 20 for each child. (Enlarge, if desired.) Help children read each sentence and have them draw a picture showing that part of the truck's journey. Invite children to decorate the mini-book cover with crayons or markers.

2. Help children cut along the dashed lines to separate the mini-book pages. Using *Truck* as a reference, help children recall the sequence of the story and have them put the pages in order behind the cover.

3. Help children staple the book together at the back end of the truck. Then have them cut off the top of the whole book, cutting along the dashed line on the cover. Let children read their truck-shaped books and share their illustrations with a partner.

Duck in the Truck
by Jez Alborough
(HarperCollins, 2000).

When Duck's truck gets stuck in the muck, will he get unstuck or is he out of luck? This rhyming story is one children will want to hear again and again.

Truck Song
by Diane Siebert
(HarperTrophy, 1987).

Through rhyming and rhythmic verse, this story follows trucks as they travel over highways and through farmlands and cities, carrying their heavy loads from one place to another.

Trucks
by Byron Barton
(HarperCollins, 1986).

From tow trucks to cement trucks to newspaper delivery trucks, this book's simple text and bright illustrations introduce children to a variety of trucking vehicles and what they do.

You Can Name 100 Trucks!
by Jim Becker
(Scholastic, 1994).

This truck-shaped board book introduces 100 different kinds of trucks and shows the many jobs they do.

The truck stopped for gas.

The truck went through a tunnel.

The tricycles were loaded onto the truck.

Truck

by _____

The tricycles were unloaded from the truck.

The truck went over a bridge.

Teaching Reading With Donald Crews Books © 2008 by Pamela Chanko, Scholastic Teaching Resources

Freight Train

(GREENWILLOW, 1978)

Inside Freight Train

(HARPERCOLLINS, 2001)

The Caldecott Honor Book *Freight Train* follows a train on its journey along the track, introducing the name and color of each car. As the train travels through tunnels and goes by cities, the blurring colors create an exciting sensation of movement—until the train whizzes out of sight and the track is empty once more. *Inside Freight Train* follows up by expanding the concepts introduced in the first book. In an innovative sliding-page format, children can actually open the doors of each car to see what freight it carries.

Concepts and Themes

▲▲▲▲▲▲

- ☼ vehicles: trains
- ☼ parts of trains, car names
- ☼ types of freight
- ☼ color words

Before Reading

Tap children's prior knowledge of trains, how they work, and what they do. Ask:

✳ Have you ever ridden on a train? Where were you going? Did the train move quickly or slowly?

✳ What can trains carry besides people? Do you think a train might carry animals, food, or toys? Why or why not?

✳ How is a train similar to and different from other vehicles, such as a car or a bus?

Invite children to list any parts of trains they know, such as wheels, engine, and cars. Then display the covers of the books and ask children to predict what each might be about. Ask:

✳ Where do you think the freight train is going? What things do you think you will find inside the cars?

After Reading

After sharing *Freight Train*, encourage children to tell what they learned by asking: "What did the freight train travel on? What kinds of places did it pass through on its trip?" Page through the book again, inviting children to supply the color word as you say the name of each car. After sharing *Inside Freight Train*, discuss the contents of the cars. Ask:

(continues)

Word Play

Use *Freight Train* to create a wall of color words. Page through the book with children and ask them to point out each color word (*red, orange, yellow, green, blue, purple,* and *black*). Then invite them to come up with additional color words, such as *pink, brown, white,* and *gray*. (They might use a box of crayons for inspiration!) Write each color word on an index card, using a color marker or crayon that matches the word. Display all the cards on a wall for children to read and use in their writing activities.

❋ What kinds of things did the freight train carry?

❋ Were there any items that surprised you?

❋ Why do you think different kinds of cars carry different items? For instance, why would fruit go in a refrigerator car?

You might also discuss with children the differences between a freight train and a passenger train: while a passenger train helps people travel, a freight train carries goods from one place to another.

Freight Sort Language Arts: Vocabulary & Social Studies

Invite children to create shoe box train cars for a freight-sorting activity.

1. After reading *Freight Train* and *Inside Freight Train*, work with children to create a list of the train car names mentioned in the books: *caboose, stock car, tank car, refrigerator car, cattle car, gondola, hopper, box car, engine,* and *tender*.

2. Gather several empty shoe boxes, one to represent each type of train car. Invite children to work in small groups to decorate the outside of each box to look like one of the cars. (They might use the books' illustrations for reference.) Label each box with the appropriate car's name.

3. Revisit the stories and help children recall what kind of freight goes in each car. Invite children to gather "freight" from around the classroom (for instance, plastic toy cows, farm animals, people, play food, small books, and toys). Children can also cut shapes from colored construction paper to represent freight (such as black ovals for coal and small brown circles for cereal). They can also create produce such as apples and peaches from play dough.

4. Once children have gathered or created a variety of freight, place the items in a large basket or tub. Then line up the shoe-box freight cars on a table. Invite children to take turns choosing an item from the basket and placing it in an appropriate car. Encourage children to explain their reasoning as they sort. You might keep the books close by so children can refer to them as they load up their train.

Freight Train Shape Search Math & Social Studies

In addition to introducing colors, the bold graphics of *Freight Train* make it a perfect venue for exploring shapes.

1. Page through the book with children, inviting them to point out any shapes they see in the illustrations. Some shapes they might find include triangles, squares, rectangles, and circles.

2. Provide children with sheets of plain white construction paper and precut shapes of different colors and sizes. Invite them to move the shapes around the paper to create their own train (for example, a large rectangle for a car, small circles for wheels, squares for windows, and an upside-down triangle for the engine car's funnel). Once their shape trains are assembled, have children glue down the pieces on their paper.

3. Have children count the number of each shape they used in their train and help them create an "answer key" on the back of their paper. (For instance: 4 circles, 2 squares, 1 rectangle, 1 triangle.)

4. When children are finished, invite them to trade shape trains with a partner. Encourage children to count the number of each shape they see, then turn the paper over to check their guesses.

Color Train Banner Art & Social Studies

Use the reproducibles on pages 25–26 to create a colorful train banner for the walls of your classroom.

1. Make one copy of the engine pattern on page 25 and a class set of the car pattern on page 26. Explain to children that they will be creating a special train—one that carries freight by color!

(continues)

Word Play

Use *Inside Freight Train* for a mini-lesson on plurals. As you slide open the pages, invite children to point out words that end in *s*. (Words they will find include *toys, books, cows, apples,* and *pears.*) Ask: "What does the *s* ending mean in each word?" (*It names more than one.*) Invite children to come up with more plurals by looking around the classroom and naming items, such as *books, desks,* and *chairs.* Write the words on the board, underlining the *s* in each one.

2. Have children work together to cut out and decorate the train engine. They might use markers or crayons to create rainbow stripes or brightly colored polka dots, sprinkle on multi-colored glitter, and so on. Glue the engine to a sheet of white construction paper, aligning the connector bar to the right edge of the paper.

3. Pass out copies of the car pattern and assign each child a color from the book (red, orange, yellow, green, blue, or purple). Assign colors as evenly as possible among children. Then help them cut out their train cars and cut along the dashed lines to create door flaps. Have children fold the flaps back and glue the car to a sheet of white construction paper, leaving the door flaps free to open and close. Trim the each side of the paper to the edge of the connector bar.

4. Ask children to close the door flaps and use crayons or markers to color their train car the assigned color. Have them write the color word on the line to complete the rhyme.

5. Have children fold back the door flaps and draw one or more items in their assigned color inside the train car. For instance, they might draw red apples, strawberries, and a sweater in the red car. Children might also cut out colored items from magazines to glue inside the car. Help children write the name of each item next to its picture and then close the doors.

6. To make the banner, attach the engine to a classroom wall. Then attach the cars in a line behind the engine to complete the train. (You might display the cars in the same color sequence shown in the book.) Invite children to read the rhyme on each train car, then open the doors to see the colored freight inside.

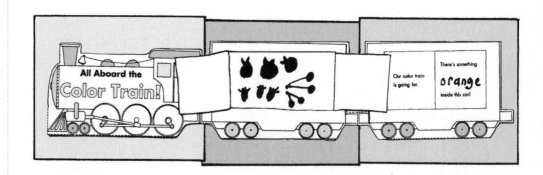

All Aboard the
Color Train!

Teaching Reading With Donald Crews Books © 2008 by Pamela Chanko, Scholastic Teaching Resources

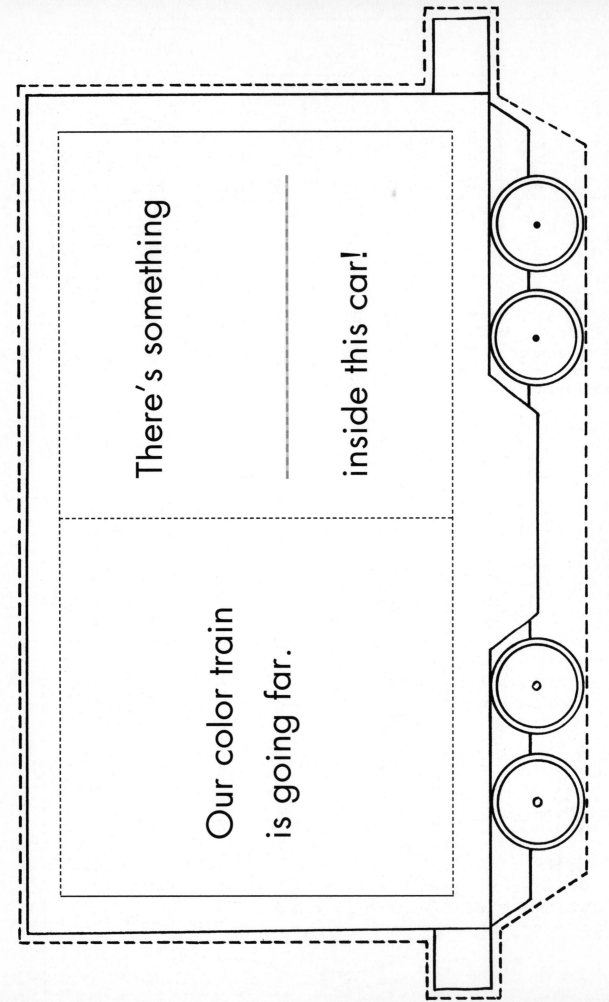

There's something

_____

inside this car!

Our color train
is going far.

Flying

◆◆

(GREENWILLOW, 1986)

From boarding to taxiing to takeoff to touchdown, this book leads children through all the steps of an airplane trip. The brilliant illustrations show a bird's-eye view of the journey as the plane flies over highways, rivers, cities, mountains, and towns. And when the plane arrives at the airport, friends and loved ones are waiting to welcome their long-distance visitors.

Before Reading

Invite children to tell what they know about airplanes and airplane travel. Ask:

* Have you ever ridden on an airplane? Where were you going? How long did it take you to get there?

* What things can you see from the window of an airplane?

* Do people use airplanes to travel short distances or longer ones? Why do you think so?

Next, tap children's prior knowledge about airports. Ask:

* Have you ever been to the airport? Were you there to get on a plane, or to pick someone up?

* What kinds of things can you see at an airport?

* What are some things people do at the airport before getting on a plane? For instance, what do they do with their suitcases?

Show children the cover of the book and invite them to make predictions about the story. Where might the airplane be going?

After Reading

Encourage children to retell the sequence of the airplane's flight by asking:

* What did the airplane passengers do first in the story? What happened next?

* What happened after the airplane left the runway? What kinds of places did the airplane fly over on its trip?

(continues)

Concepts and Themes

▲▲▲▲▲▲▲

☼ vehicles: airplanes

☼ airports

☼ flight

☼ long-distance travel

Word Play

- Use the book for a mini-lesson on positional words. Point out the line "Flying over the airport" and ask: "What part of this sentence tells where the plane is flying?" (*over the airport*) Then do the same for "Flying across the country" and "Flying into the clouds." Write *over*, *across*, and *into* on the board, explaining that these words tell where something is.

  Work with children to brainstorm more positional words and phrases, such as *under*, *next to*, *behind*, and *near*. You might use a paper airplane to demonstrate each positional concept in a sentence (for instance, *The plane is* under *the desk*).

- Point out that sometimes print itself can hint about where something is or where it is going. Turn to the second-to-last page and point out the words "Down, down, down." Discuss with children how the words are placed on the page to show how the plane is landing.

✳ Were you surprised to see that the airplane flew through a cloud? What do you think the cloud looked like from inside the plane?

✳ What did the passengers do after the plane landed? Who do you think the people were who were waiting for them?

Invite children who have ridden on airplanes to share their experiences and compare them with the flight shown in the story. What does it feel like to take off, taxi, and touch down? Did the illustrations accurately show how things look from the window of an airplane?

Wind Beneath My Wings Science

How do an airplane's wings help it stay in the air? Do this quick and easy experiment to find out.

1. Provide children with 3- by 11-inch strips of paper. Help them fold the strip in half and make a crease. Then help children tape the top edge of the paper about one inch from the bottom edge. This will create a wing shape with a curved top and a flat bottom.

2. Next, have children slide a ruler into the fold of the paper. Show children how to hold the ruler in front of them horizontally and blow toward the fold. What happens to the wing when the air hits it? (*The wing rises into the air.*)

3. To lay the foundation for a deep understanding in later grades, explain to children that this is how real airplane wings are shaped: they are curved at the top and flat on the bottom. This means that the air has to go faster over the top of the wing than the bottom, creating more air pressure on the bottom of the wing. This pressure gives the plane "lift" and keeps it up in the air.

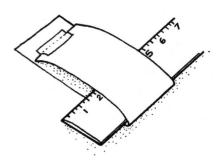

Look! Up in the Air! Science & Social Studies

What do airplanes have in common with other things that fly? Help children use a Venn diagram to show what they know.

1. Help children brainstorm a list of things—in addition to airplanes—that fly, such as birds, butterflies, bees, and bats. Write each item on a large index card.

2. Then generate a list of attributes for planes, and for each additional thing that flies. Write these words on additional cards. Words might include *wings*, *body*, *wheels*, *windows*, *feet*, *antennae*, *eyes*, and so on.

3. Place two hula hoops (or large yarn circles) on the floor so that they intersect. Place the "Airplane" card above one hoop and a card for another thing that flies (such as "Bird") above the second circle. Give children the attribute cards and help them place them in the appropriate sections on the diagram. Attributes belonging only to airplanes should go in the first circle, attributes belonging only to birds should go in the second circle, and attributes belonging to both should go in the intersection. Any attributes belonging to neither item should be placed outside the diagram.

4. Continue comparing planes to other things that fly by placing different cards above the second circle. Encourage children to explain their reasoning as they place the attribute cards in the diagram.

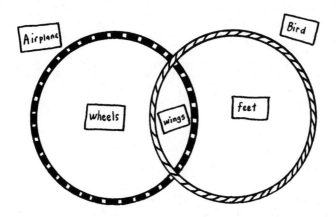

Build a Flying Machine Science

Invite children to design their own airplane from scrap materials.

1. Provide children with aluminum foil, pieces of cardboard, pipe cleaners, wood scraps, and so on. You might also provide children with pictures of different kinds of airplanes from books and magazines to use as references as they work.

2. Children can scrunch and crumple the foil into different shapes to create their plane's body and tail, glue cardboard wings to the sides, and add large wooden beads to the bottom for wheels.

3. When they have finished, encourage children to write their name and the name of their plane on an index card. Display the creations in an "Aviation Museum" and encourage each designer to describe his or her work, telling what each part of the machine is for.

Airport
by Lola M. Schaefer
(Heinemann, 2000).

From the customer service agent to the air traffic specialist, meet all the people who work to keep the airport running smoothly.

Amazing Airplanes
by Tony Mitton
(Houghton Mifflin, 2002).

Rhyming text introduces children to the many aspects of air travel, from how planes fly to safety rules to in-flight entertainment.

Angela's Airplane
by Robert Munsch
(Annick, 1988).

When Angela and her father get separated at the airport, she finds herself in the front of the plane. She decides to push just one button. . . and the adventure begins!

First Flight
by David McPhail
(Little Brown, 1991).

Flying alone for the first time can be scary. But when a little boy takes his teddy bear on his first solo flight, it's the bear who needs reassurance from his traveling companion.

Let's Travel! Tickets & Postcards
Writing, Reading & Social Studies

Invite children to create a ticket for a fantasy airplane trip and send a postcard from their destination!

1. Talk with children about a place they would like to travel to on an airplane. It might be a place they have been to before, such as the home of a relative, a place they would like to visit (such as a far-away country), or even a magical place from a favorite story or their own imaginations.

2. Give each child a copy of the reproducible on page 31. Help children cut out the airplane ticket and postcard. Then assist them in completing the information on their tickets by writing their name, flight number, date, their hometown or city, and the name of the place they are traveling to. Also help children invent departure and arrival times for their flight.

3. To create the postcard, have children fold down the middle and seal with a glue stick. Encourage children to draw a picture of the place they are visiting on the front of the card and write the place name on the line. On the back of the card, children can write a message to someone back home telling what they are doing on their trip. Have children draw a stamp and fill in the address lines.

4. Once children's tickets and postcards are complete, they can be used for dramatic play activities. Invite children to use their tickets to board a "plane" and act out their fantasy trip. Children can then "send" their postcards to classmates telling all about their adventures!

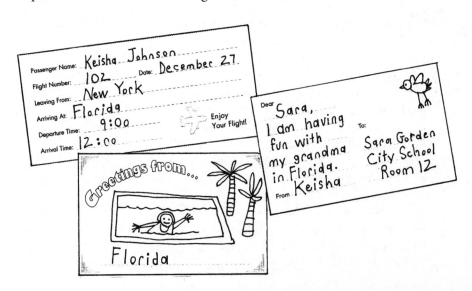

Passenger Name: _____

Flight Number: _____ Date: _____

Leaving From: _____

Arriving At: _____

Departure Time: _____

Arrival Time: _____

Enjoy Your Flight!

From

Dear

To:

Greetings from...

Harbor

(GREENWILLOW, 1982)

Sail Away

(HARPERTROPHY, 1995)

Concepts and Themes

▲▲▲▲▲▲

- ☼ vehicles: water transportation

- ☼ boats and ships, harbors

- ☼ seas, waves

In these books, children learn all about water transportation. *Harbor* introduces a busy port full of ferries, liners, tankers, tugboats, freighters, barges, and much more. Each boat has a different shape and a different function. *Sail Away* focuses on recreational water transport, as children follow a family on a day of sailing through both calm and angry seas. Whether they are used to transport cargo, passengers, or just for fun, boats are amazing vehicles!

Before Reading

Tap children's prior knowledge about boats. Ask:

- ✳ What do boats travel on? How are boats different from other kinds of vehicles, such as trains, cars, or trucks?

- ✳ What are some different types of boats? How about a ferry, a sailboat, or a tugboat? Have you ever seen any of these boats? What do they look like?

- ✳ Have you ever been on a boat? What kind of boat was it? Did you use the boat to get from one place to another, or were you just riding on it for fun?

- ✳ Can boats carry things besides people? What kinds of cargo do you think a boat might hold?

Show children the cover of each book and read both titles aloud. Invite children to compare the boats on each cover by asking:

- ✳ How are these two boats alike? How are they different?

- ✳ If you could take a ride on either boat, which would you choose and why?

After Reading

After reading *Harbor*, turn to the glossary in the back and review the name of each boat. Then page through the book again, challenging children to find each one. Encourage children to describe the function of each boat:

- ✳ What do you think the ferry is used for? Why doesn't it need to turn around when it goes back and forth?

✳ What was the long barge carrying?

✳ Why is the tugboat "the busiest boat in the harbor"? What is its job?

After reading *Sail Away*, ask:

✳ How was the boat in this book different from the boats in *Harbor*? What did the people use the boat for? What made the boat move?

✳ What happened when the weather changed? Why might it be difficult to sail through a storm?

Invite children who have been on different kinds of boats (such as ferries, cruise ships, sailboats, or rowboats) to share their experiences. How is traveling on each kind of boat the same? How is it different?

Sink or Float? Science

Introduce children to the concept of buoyancy with a simple hands-on experiment.

1. Fill your water table or a large tub with water. Gather objects to test, such as several different coins, a Ping-Pong ball, a cork, a bar of soap, marbles, a unit block, and small plastic toys. Place the items in a large paper bag. Create a two-column chart labeled "Our Prediction" and "Results." Write the name of each object down the left side of the chart.

2. Invite one child to reach into the bag and pick an item. Pass the item around, inviting children to make observations. What shape is the item? How heavy is it? Ask, "What will happen when we place the [name of object] in water? Will it sink or will it float? Ask children to explain the reasoning for their predictions. Then write the majority prediction next to the item's name in the first column on the chart.

3. Next, place the object in the water and observe what happens. Write the results in the second column. Continue your experiment by letting children take turns removing an item from the bag, making predictions, and testing the item. When finished, look at your completed chart with the group and discuss the results. How accurate were children's predictions? What did the "sinkers" have in common? How about the "floaters"?

4. Young children may think that the *buoyancy* (capacity to float) of an item depends upon its weight. However, the object's *density* (how compact it is—how much space its weight takes up) is the key factor at work. Try this: Test a small ball of clay. (*It sinks.*) Challenge children to try to change the shape of the clay so that it will float. (When the clay is molded into a boat shape, for example, it has more surface area for the water to push upward; therefore, it floats.)

Use *Harbor* for a mini-lesson on compound words. Point out the word *ferryboats* and ask: "What two small words can you find in this big word?" (*ferry, boats*) Explain that this is a compound word, and ask children to hunt for more compound words in the book (*warehouses, tugboats, fireboat*). Write each word on the board, drawing a line to separate the two smaller words. Then ask children to come up with more compound words, such as *sidewalk, firefly, ladybug,* and *airplane*. You might like to write each word on an index card to create a word wall.

	Our Prediction	Results
block	sink	sink
cork	float	float
penny	float	sink

Word Play

- Use *Sail Away* to introduce children to onomatopoeia—words that imitate sounds. Point out the repeated use of "putt...putt... putt" throughout the book. Ask, "What does this word mean?" (*It is the sound the boat's motor makes.*) "What is another sound that a boat or other vehicle might make?" (*toot, beep, vroom*)

  Write each word on the board and spark ideas for additional words by asking questions such as: "What sound does a bee make?" (*buzz*) "What sound does a potato chip make in your mouth?" (*crunch*)

- Tell children that not only can words sound like what they mean— they can also look like what they mean! Return to the book and turn the pages slowly, asking children to point out unusual styles of print. Call attention to the large, slanted *whoosh* that shows the wind, and point out how the print gets larger and slants in different ways to show the storm.

Make a Balloon Boat Science

Explore two kinds of air power with a balloon boat.

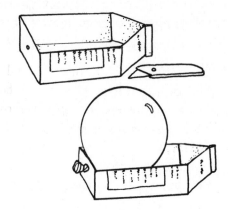

1. To make a boat, use a craft knife to cut a clean, empty half-gallon milk carton in half lengthwise. (Keep the craft knife out of children's reach.) Poke a small hole in the center of the flat end of the boat. Then, to make a "sail," thread the lip of a balloon through the hole, blow up the balloon, and tie it closed with a loose knot.

2. Set your balloon boat out to "sea" in a water table or large tub filled with water. How can children make the boat move? Explain that the balloon acts as a sail. Invite children to take turns blowing the balloon sail gently, and then hard, to create different speeds of wind. You might also use an electric fan to create wind (use caution when operating the fan near water). How does the boat move when air is blown at it at different speeds? How about different directions?

3. After experimenting with wind, tell children that they can change their sailboat to a jet-powered boat! To demonstrate, untie the balloon, holding the lip closed tightly to keep the air inside. Then place the boat in the water and release the balloon. The force of the air leaving the balloon will "jet" the boat across the water!

Boat Book Reading, Writing & Social Studies

Help children research different types of boats for a collaborative class book.

1. Brainstorm a list of different types of boats with children, such as sailboats, rowboats, tugboats, ferries, and freighters. (You might look at the glossary in the back of *Harbor* for additional ideas.)

2. Divide the class into pairs or small groups and assign each a different type of boat. Help children find facts about their boats using library books, encyclopedias, or the Internet. Topics of interest might include what makes the boat move (sails and wind, an engine, oars or paddles, steam), what the boat is used for (to carry passengers, ship cargo, tow other boats, keep the harbor safe), and what people help run the boat (a captain, rowers, firefighters).

3. Have children work together to draw a picture of their boat and write or dictate facts they found. Let the class work together to design a cover. Bind the pages together with yarn, then add the completed book to your classroom library. Encourage children to share their pages with the class and tell what they learned about boats.

Making Waves Science

In *Sail Away*, a change in the weather caused choppy seas and a rough ride. How does wind help create waves? Try this activity to find out.

1. Fill a rectangular glass pan (such as a casserole dish) half-full with water. Place a few drops of food coloring in the water, without stirring it.

2. Invite a volunteer to blow on the water, trying to make the food coloring move. Have additional children join the first volunteer, making the "wind" stronger and stronger. Ask, "What happens to the water? What happens to the food coloring?" (*The water begins to ripple and the color begins to move with it.*)

3. Encourage children to imagine that the color in the water was a sailboat. "How might a strong wind affect the boat? Why might it be more difficult to sail in rough waves than in calmer water?"

Book Links

The Boat Alphabet Book
by Jerry Pallotta
(Charlesbridge, 2003).

From an aircraft carrier to an inflatable zodiac, children learn about all kinds of vessels as they take an unusual voyage through the ABC's.

I'm Mighty!
by Kate McMullan
(HarperCollins, 2003).

The tugboat may look small, but it has the biggest job in the harbor! Children will enjoy hearing this scrappy little hero describe his mighty deeds.

Sheep on a Ship
by Nancy E. Shaw
(Houghton Mifflin, 1992).

Follow the rhyming adventures of a flock of zany sheep as they brave a storm and save their ship's treasure.

Who Sank the Boat?
by Pamela Allen
(Putnam, 1996).

When a cow, a donkey, a sheep, a pig, and a tiny mouse decide to go for a row in the bay, children are invited to guess the answer to the title's question.

Ten Black Dots

❖❖

(GREENWILLOW, 1986)

Concepts and Themes

▲▲▲▲▲▲

☀ numbers, numerals 1–10

☀ counting

☀ shapes: circles

☀ colors: black

☀ rhyming words

What can you do with ten black dots? In this innovative book, children see that one dot can make a sun, two can make the eyes of a fox, three can make a snowman's face... and that's just the beginning! Rhyming text and bold illustrations introduce children to the numbers one to ten in a whole new way.

Before Reading

Show children the cover of the book and read the title aloud. Invite children to count with you as you point to each black dot. Ask:

✳ How many dots are there all together? What shape are the dots? What color?

✳ What numeral do you see on the cover?

✳ What other numbers do you think you will see in this book?

✳ Can you name any items that have black dots? How about a Dalmatian dog or a ladybug?

✳ What pictures do you think the author will make out of the dots in this book?

You might also prepare for reading by tapping children's prior knowledge of the numbers 1–10. Discuss things that come in ones (nose, hat) twos (eyes, mittens), and so on up to tens (fingers, toes).

After Reading

After reading the book once with children, page through it again, this time asking them to count the dots on each page and supply the number word as you read. Then help children retell the numerical sequence of the story by asking:

✳ What did one black dot make a picture of? How about two black dots?

✳ Why do you think the author put the numbers and pictures in the order he did?

✳ Were there any pictures that surprised you? What other things might you create from one, two, or three black dots?

You might also point out that the numeral on each page is spelled out. To reinforce this concept, create a three-column chart showing the numeral, number word, and appropriate amount of dots for each number in the book.

Black Dot Counting Book Reading & Writing

After reading the book, invite children to create their own collaborative version of *Ten Black Dots*.

1. Write the following incomplete sentence on the bottom of a sheet of paper and make a copy for each child: _____ *black dots can make _____*. Provide children with a supply of precut black construction paper circles and assign each child a number from 1 to 10, distributing the numbers as evenly as possible.

2. Have children count out their assigned number of dots and invite them to use their imagination to think of a picture they might create from them. For instance, one black dot might become the center of a sunflower, two black dots might become the scoops on an ice cream cone, and three black dots might become the eyes and nose of a teddy bear. Have children glue their dots on the paper and draw around them with crayons to complete the picture.

3. Next, help children fill in the numeral and the name of the item they drew to complete the sentence. (Children doing a number *1* page can cross out the *s* in *dots* so that their sentence reads correctly.)

4. When children are finished, collect their pages and put them in numerical order (depending on the number of children in your class, you may have two or more pages for each numeral). Bind the sheets together and add the book to your classroom library. Invite children to read their new book together, count the dots, and celebrate their classmates' creativity!

Word Family Circles Reading: Phonics

You can use the rhymes in the book to begin a collection of word family "dots."

1. Cut several large circles from black craft paper or tagboard and attach them to a bulletin board or classroom wall.

2. Read the book aloud to children, inviting them to raise their hands every time they hear a rhyme. Introduce the concept of word families —words that rhyme and end with the same spelling pattern—by paging through the book again, this time inviting children to look for

(continues)

Return to the book, calling attention to the page about three dots. Point out the word *snowman's* and ask children what they notice between the *n* and the *s* (*an apostrophe*). Explain that in this case, the apostrophe shows that something belongs to the snowman—his face. Then use a child's name in the possessive, pointing out a different body part, such as *Peter's arm* or *Deirdre's nose*. Invite children to practice the structure by pointing to things that belong to them, for instance, *Moshe's book*, *Geraldo's backpack*, and so on.

rhyming word pairs that end with the same group of letters. As children find word family pairs, write each word on a white index card. (Word pairs in the book include *face/lace, coat/boat, hold/old, rank/bank, train/rain, snake/rake,* and *tree/free*.)

3. Begin your word family circles by attaching each pair of rhyming words to a separate black dot. Then invite children to suggest an additional word with the same spelling pattern to attach to each dot (for instance, *race, goat, cold, tank, plain, cake,* and *bee*). If children suggest words that rhyme but do not have a matching spelling pattern, explain that some words sound the same but are spelled differently.

4. Continue to add to your word family circles as children suggest new words. You might also create additional dots for other common word families, such as *-at, -in,* and *-ock.*

Black Dot Snacks

1 heaping cup flour
1/2 teaspoon baking powder
1/2 cup white sugar
1/2 cup brown sugar
1 stick butter, softened

1 teaspoon vanilla
6 ounces chocolate chips
    (or substitute black raisins)
1/2 cup bran flakes
1 egg

1. Help children measure and mix all the ingredients in a large bowl and stir together.
2. Spread the mixture into a 9- by 13-inch pan.
3. Bake at 350° F for approximately 20 minutes.
4. Let cool and cut into snack-sized squares.
5. Eat up and enjoy—and don't forget to count each black dot in your snack!

Yummy Black Dot Snacks Cooking & Math

What's the tastiest kind of black dot there is? Chocolate chips, of course! Work with children to prepare this easy-to-make recipe. Then serve the snacks at snack time or as a follow-up to a counting activity. Now that's a delicious snack you can count on! (Check for food allergies ahead of time.)

I Spy...Dots! Language Arts

Circle shapes are all around us. Help children recognize them with a guessing game. Gather children together and begin the game with your own "I Spy" clue about a circle in the classroom. For instance: "I spy a circle on the wall with numbers and two hands. It tells us what time it is." Encourage children to look around the room and guess the "secret circle" (classroom clock). Follow with additional clues about circles in the classroom, such as toy car wheels, a doorknob, or even the sun outside your window. Once children are familiar with the game, invite them to take turns making up their own circle clues for the group to guess.

Black Dot Number Match Cards

Math

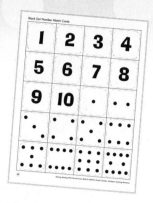

Use the cards on page 40 to create a variety of number-matching games. Make several copies of the activity sheet and cut the cards apart on the dashed lines. Following are a few games to try:

◎ **Numeral Match Dominoes:** Draw a line down the center of several index cards. Glue one numeral card and one dot card on each side of the line in random order. You can create as many dominoes as you like. To play, divide the dominoes evenly among a small group of children. Have one child set out a domino. The next player tries to make a match with one side of one of his or her dominoes by matching the numeral to the number of dots. Children continue to take turns setting out dominoes until no more matches can be made. The first player to use all of his or her dominoes (or the player who has the fewest left) wins the game.

◎ **Concentration:** Cut out one set of dot and numeral cards for each pair of children. Glue each card to a plain index card. To play, have children mix up the cards and lay them face down. The first player turns over any two cards. If one card has a number of dots that matches the numeral on the other, the player keeps the pair. If not, the cards are turned back over. Children take turns until each card has been matched with its partner. The player with the most cards at the end of the game wins.

◎ **Find a Partner:** Glue each card to an index card, punch a hole through the top, and string with yarn to make a necklace. Give each child a necklace, making sure he or she has a partner with a matching card. (If working with more than 20 students, create additional cards. For instance, if you have 22 children, create one card with the numeral 11 and one with 11 black dots.) Have children put on their necklaces with the numeral or dots facing in. When you say "Find your match!" children turn their cards over and find the child with the matching card. You can use this game as a way to pair up children for partnered activities, to line up children with buddies for going outdoors, and so on.

Book Links

Fish Eyes: A Book You Can Count On by Lois Ehlert (Harcourt, 1990).

In this colorful book, children count from one to ten in a different way—by taking a journey under the sea and counting the eyes on a school of fanciful fish.

Mouse Count by Ellen Stoll Walsh (Harcourt, 1995).

This charming counting book tells the story of ten very smart mice who outwit a hungry snake.

One Was Johnny: A Counting Book by Maurice Sendak (HarperCollins, 1990).

Children will enjoy counting along from one to ten and back again as they follow the adventures of Johnny and all the unwelcome visitors who come to call— and see how he gets rid of them all!

Ten, Nine, Eight by Molly Bang (HarperCollins, 1983).

This gentle, lilting story counts down the nightly rituals of a parent and child at bedtime, from "ten small toes all washed and warm" to "one big girl all ready for bed."

Black Dot Number Match Cards

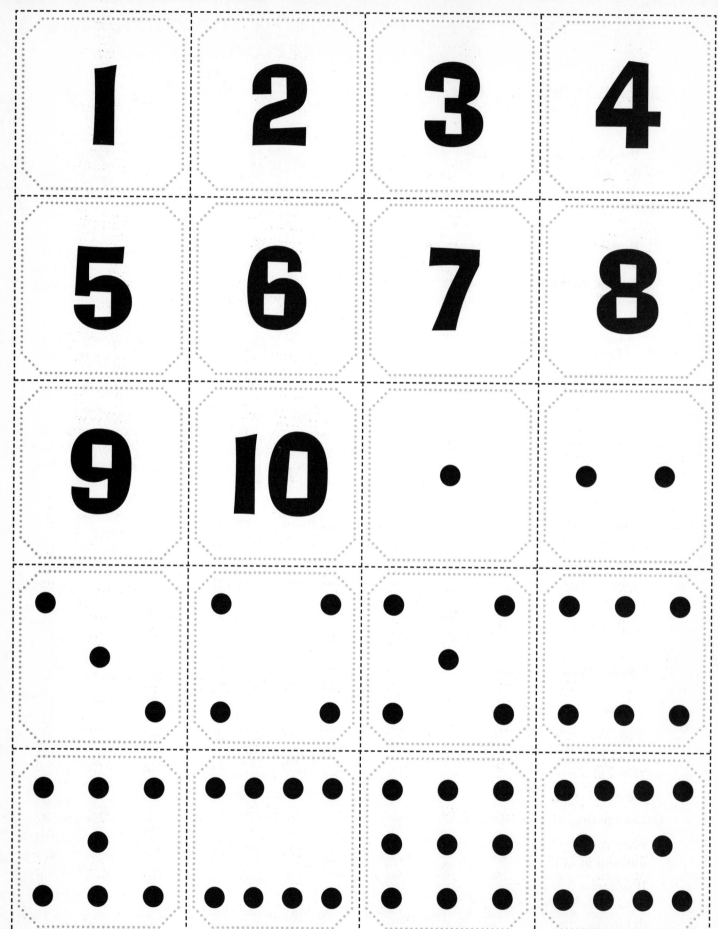

Bicycle Race

(GREENWILLOW, 1985)

There's a bicycle race today, and all twelve riders are ready to go. But wait! When the race begins, number nine is in trouble and needs a bike repair. The race progresses, and the numbered order of the riders changes as some pull ahead and others fall behind. Will number nine catch up in time to win the race? Children will enjoy being spectators of this exciting contest as they learn numeral recognition.

Concepts and Themes

- ☼ numbers, numerals 1–12
- ☼ bicycles
- ☼ sports
- ☼ races, competition

Before Reading

Begin by tapping children's prior knowledge of bicycles. Ask:

* Do you know how to ride a bicycle or a tricycle? How did you learn to do it? Did someone teach you? How did you feel when you did it for the first time by yourself?

* How do you make a bicycle go? What are the pedals used for? How about the wheels?

* What are some important safety rules to follow when riding a bicycle? Is there any special equipment you should wear? How does a helmet help keep you safe?

Next, show children the cover of the book and read the title aloud. Ask:

* How many cyclists do you see on the cover? How many riders do you think will be in the race? Who do you think will win?

After Reading

Invite children to retell the sequence of the story by asking:

* What happened when the race began? Which rider was in trouble? What was wrong?

* Why did the order of the numbers keep changing during the race?

* Were you surprised when rider number nine won the race? Why or why not?

Encourage children to relate the story to their own experiences. Ask:

* Have you ever been in a race or watched a race? Was it a bicycle race or a different kind of sport? What was it like? Was it exciting?

* If you were in a bicycle race and something happened to your bike, how would you solve the problem? Would you keep on trying, as number nine did in the story?

Word Play

Bicycle Race provides a great opportunity to create a number words wall. Page back through the book with children, asking them to point out each word that names a number. Point out the difference between a numeral (*2*) and a number word (*two*). In addition, point out that the number words are not in regular order; instead, they are in the order that shows which rider is ahead in the race. (Children may also notice that the print slants and curves on the pages, as if it is following the path of the race, too.)

Once you have found all the number words in the book, write each one on an index card and attach it to a wall or bulletin board. Then create index cards with the matching numerals, and post them on the board in mixed-up order. Children can practice word recognition by matching each numeral to the correct number word.

Numeral Scavenger Hunt Math

Numbers are everywhere! Help children find and recognize them with a scavenger hunt game.

1. Create a record sheet by writing the numerals 0–9 down the left side of a sheet of paper and make a copy for each child.

2. Gather children together and distribute the sheets. Help them name each numeral and ask where they might find numbers in the classroom. Ideas might include the classroom clock, a calendar, a daily schedule, or even the room number on your door.

3. When children are ready, send them off on the scavenger hunt. Have them make a tally mark next to each numeral they find. Explain that a two-digit number counts as two numerals. For instance, if children find a "10," they should make one mark next to the "1" and one mark next to the "0" on their sheets.

4. When children are finished, gather together and compare results. Which numeral did children find the most of? In what kinds of places did children find numerals?

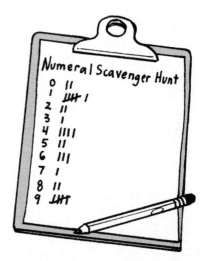

Variation: To turn the scavenger hunt into a racing game, divide the class into pairs or small groups and assign each a different numeral on the sheet. Designate a time period for the scavenger hunt race, such as ten minutes. When you say "Go!" have children begin hunting for as many examples of their assigned numeral as they can find. When time is up, the group with the most tally marks on their sheet wins the race.

My Dream Bike Art & Writing

Turn bicycle riding into a magical adventure with a creative art activity.

1. Discuss with children the features commonly found on bicycles: wheels, pedals, handlebars, and so on. How is each part of the bicycle used? How does it help the rider make the bike move?

2. Provide children with paper, crayons, markers, and collage materials such as old magazines, foil, glitter, and fabric scraps. Invite children to

use the materials to create a picture of their "dream bike." What special features would their bicycle have? Would it include a musical instrument instead of a bicycle bell? Wings to make the bicycle fly? Would the bicycle be formed in an unusual shape, such as a dinosaur or a butterfly? Invite children to be creative and let their imaginations soar!

My dream bike looks like a bird. It can fly!

3. When children are finished with their creations, help them write or dictate a sentence telling about what unusual features their dream bicycle has and what special things it can do. Display children's work on a classroom wall and invite them to invent adventure stories about each other's dream vehicles.

Fun on Wheels Social Studies

What are some ways to have fun on wheels? Create a four-column chart on a large sheet of tagboard or chart paper. Then invite children to find out.

1. Brainstorm with children various sports and activities that involve wheels, such as bicycle or tricycle riding, rollerblading or roller-skating, skateboarding, and riding on a scooter. Write the name of each activity in the first column on the chart.

2. Use the next column for pictures of each type of equipment. Children can find pictures of bicycles, skates, and skateboards in magazines, or draw their own.

3. Invite children to describe how to do each activity. Write their ideas in the third column next to each picture. Finally, discuss additional equipment needed for each sport, such as a helmet, kneepads, and wrist guards. Write this information in the last column.

4. When the chart is complete, review the information together. How are the various activities different from one another? What things do they have in common? You might use this opportunity to discuss important safety guidelines, such as wearing the appropriate protective equipment and following the rules of the road.

5. Extend your exploration into a graphing activity. Write the names of the sports across the top of the board and have children make tally marks under the activities they have tried, the activities they would like to try, or the one they enjoy most. Graph and discuss the results as a class.

Book Links

Bicycle Book
by Gail Gibbons
(Holiday House, 1995).

This book provides a history of bicycles, the science of how they work, and safety tips for riders.

Curious George Rides a Bike
by H. A. Rey
(Houghton Mifflin, 1973).

Everyone's favorite monkey is up to his usual mischief once more—this time on wheels!

D.W. Rides Again!
by Marc Brown
(Little Brown, 1996).

When the spunky D.W. trades in her tricycle for a two-wheeler, her big brother Arthur steps in to provide a much-needed lesson in bicycle riding and safety.

Franklin Rides a Bike
by Paulette Bourgeois
(Scholastic, 1997).

When Franklin is the last of his friends to need training wheels, he is determined to learn how to ride without them. After several spills and a lot of hard work, the lovable turtle finally finds success.

Bicycle Race Game Reading & Math

In the book, the numbered order of the twelve bicycle riders keeps changing as the race moves along. Challenge children to practice numeral and number word recognition as well as number sequencing skills with this game.

1. Make one copy of the game board on page 45 and the game cube on page 46 for each group (the game can be played by 2–4 players). If desired, enlarge the number cube, then assemble it as shown. Copy one set of the game cards on page 46 for each player in the group and cut them out. Provide each player with a game marker (such as different colored buttons).

2. Teach children how to play the game as follows:

- Shuffle all the sets of game cards together and place them facedown on the game board box marked "Place Cards Here." Turn over the top card and place it face up on the box marked "Discard Cards Here." Each player places a marker on a different "Go!" space on the board.

- Players take turns rolling the number cube to see how many spaces to move around the board. Each player follows any written directions on the space he or she lands on. If a player lands on a bicycle rider, he or she can either take a card from the stack of facedown cards, or take the top card off the discard pile.

- The object of the game is to collect all 12 game cards in the correct sequence. In order for a player to keep a card, it must be the one he or she needs on that turn. (The first card each player needs is rider 1, the second card must be rider 2, and so on.)

- If a player draws a needed game card, the player places it face up along his or her side of the game board.

- If not, the card must be placed face up on the discard pile and the next player takes a turn.

- The first player to collect and place all of his or her game cards in order (from 1–12) wins the game.

Leveling Tip: To simplify the game, start by using cards 1–6 only. You can then work up to 12 as children become more familiar with the game.

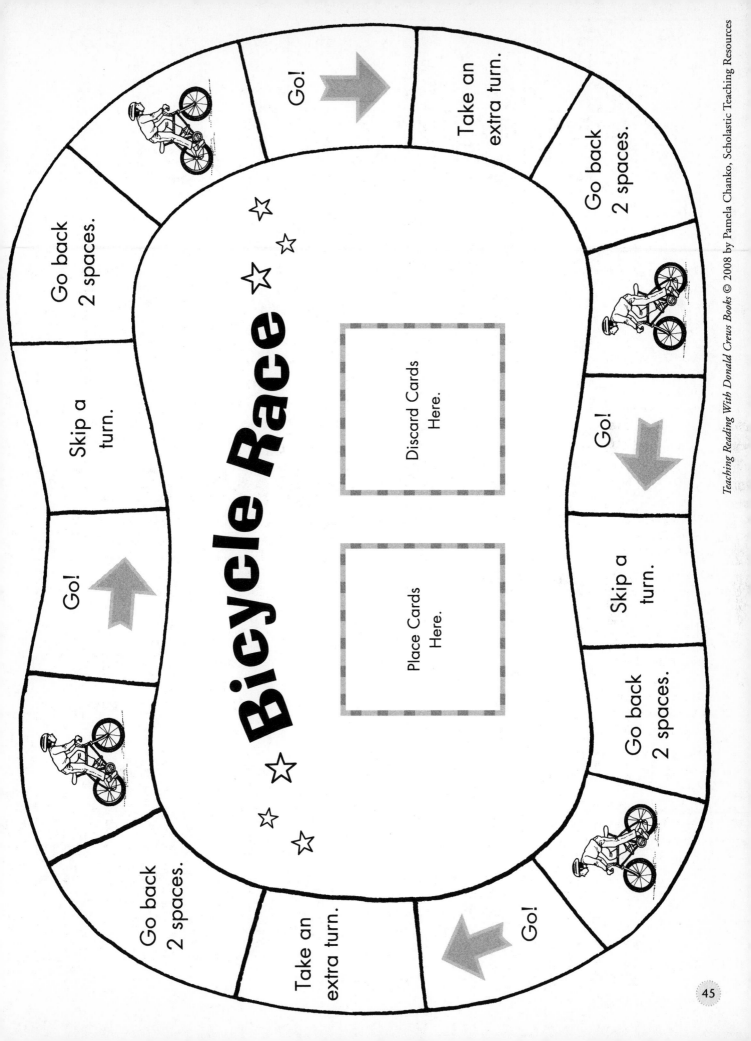

Bicycle Race

Go!

Take an extra turn.

Go back 2 spaces.

Go back 2 spaces.

Skip a turn.

Go!

Go!

Skip a turn.

Go back 2 spaces.

Go back 2 spaces.

Take an extra turn.

Go!

Discard Cards Here.

Place Cards Here.

Teaching Reading With Donald Crews Books © 2008 by Pamela Chanko, Scholastic Teaching Resources

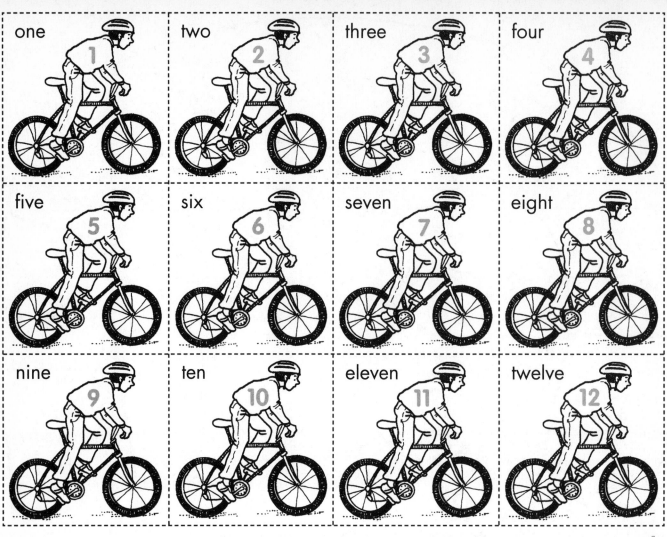

one 1	two 2	three 3	four 4
five 5	six 6	seven 7	eight 8
nine 9	ten 10	eleven 11	twelve 12

Bicycle Race Game

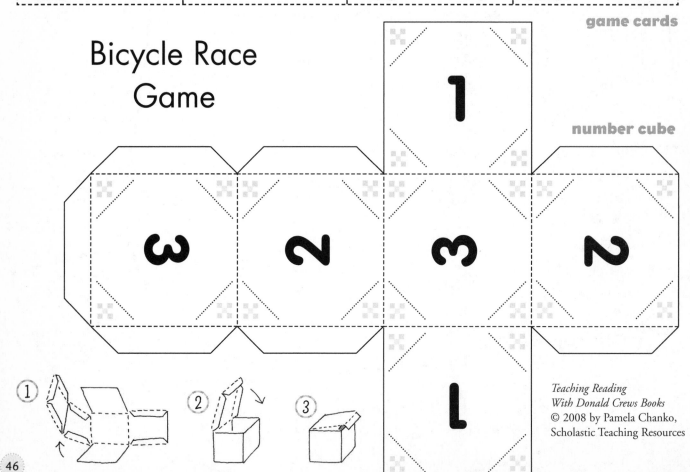

*Teaching Reading
With Donald Crews Books*
© 2008 by Pamela Chanko,
Scholastic Teaching Resources

Parade

◆◆

(GREENWILLOW, 1983)

The vendors are selling balloons, hot dogs, ice cream, and pretzels. The crowd is gathering. Here comes the parade! First come the flags, then the marching band with their many instruments. Next come the floats and the baton twirlers. And last but not least, a brand new fire engine brings up the rear. When the parade is over, the crowd disperses, and the sanitation truck arrives. It's time to clean up!

Before Reading

Invite children to tell about any experiences they may have had with parades. Ask:

* Have you ever seen a parade? What was the celebration for? Was the parade on a special holiday? What was the holiday?

* What kinds of things can you see in a parade? How about a marching band, special balloons, flags, or floats?

* Have you ever been in a parade yourself? What did you do in the parade? Did you march, play an instrument, or wear a costume? How did it feel to be in the parade? Was it exciting?

* What is the best part of a parade? Do you like the music? The decorations?

Next, show children the cover of the book and invite them to make predictions about the story. Ask:

* What kinds of things do you think you will see in this parade? What do you think the parade is for?

After Reading

Invite children to retell the sequence of the story by asking:

* What came first in the parade? What came after the flags?

* What kinds of instruments did the marching band play? What do you think the music sounded like?

* What came last in the parade?

* What happened when the parade was over?

Then invite children to relate to the story by asking:

* If you could be a part of the parade in the book, what would you most like to do? (*play with the band, twirl a baton, ride on a float*) Why?

Concepts and Themes

▲▲▲▲▲▲

☼ parades

☼ celebrations

☼ musical instruments

☼ flags

Word Play

You can use *Parade* to expand children's vocabulary with musical words. Revisit the book with children, asking them to hunt for words that name musical instruments. (Words they might find include *trombones, clarinets, saxophones,* and *cymbals.*) Write each word on the board and then ask children to name other instruments they may have heard of, such as *piano, violin,* and *tuba.* Children can use the list to write a poem or short story about a musical performance.

Join the Band! Music & Movement

Invite children to make simple rhythm instruments and form a marching band. Following are a few ideas to try.

◉ Pour a teaspoon of rice, beans, or sand into a deflated balloon. Blow up the balloon, tie it shut, and shake to play.

◉ Pour some dry macaroni into a flour sifter. Tape a piece of heavy paper over the top and shake to play.

◉ Use two saucepan lids as cymbals. Clang together to play.

◉ Sew jingle bells to the fingers of a pair of gloves. Clap hands to play.

◉ Use two cardboard tubes as rhythm sticks. Rub or tap together to play.

When children have chosen and created an instrument, let the parade begin! Play lively music (Sousa marches work well) and let children march around the classroom as they play with the band.

Shoe Box Floats Art & Writing

Children can create their own floats for a shoe box parade.

1. First, decide on a theme for your parade. It might be an upcoming holiday, a parade of favorite story characters, or simply a celebration of working and playing together at school.

2. Divide the class into small groups and give each an empty shoe box. Invite children to work together to decorate the outside of their box. They can paint the box to look like the home of a story character, glue on crumpled pieces of tissue paper in appropriate colors for the theme (for instance, orange and black for a Halloween parade), or decorate the box with any materials they choose, such as pictures cut from magazines, felt or fabric scraps, and glitter.

3. Invite children to select classroom items to put inside their shoe boxes, such as stuffed animals or toy people from the block center. Children can dress up their float-riders to look like story characters or add festive holiday gear such as special construction-paper hats. Finally, help children staple a long string of yarn to one end of the box.

4. Now have a parade! Group members can take turns pulling the floats around the classroom. You might even march your floats around the school, inviting other classes to come watch the parade.

5. Afterward, in a shared writing activity, invite children to write a collaborative story about their parade, using descriptive words to tell about each float.

Class Flags Art & Social Studies

In the book, parade marchers carry flags from many different countries. Invite children to design their own flags representing your classroom community.

1. Begin by turning to the flag illustrations in *Parade* and examining them with children. Ask:

- Can you pick out the United States flag?
- What other countries are represented in the parade?
- What does each flag look like?

You might show children pictures of additional flags from around the world. How is each flag different? Explain that every country has a special flag. Each flag uses different colors and symbols to say something about the country it represents. For instance, our country's flag has 50 stars to represent the 50 states.

2. When children have had a chance to explore several flags, invite small groups to design their own flag representing your classroom community. Provide children with large sheets of plain white construction paper, paints, crayons, and markers. Help children brainstorm symbols for their flags that say something about your class. For instance, a book might show that children love to read, a tree might show that they love to play outdoors, or a heart might show that they love being friends!

3. When children are finished, attach each flag to a dowel stick. Children can wave their flags proudly in a parade, or you can display them on the walls of the classroom. Encourage groups to describe their flags and tell what their designs and symbols mean to them.

Patterns On Parade Art and Math

Help children practice patterning skills with the activity sheet on page 51.

1. Give a copy of page 51 to each child. Help children cut out the strips and glue them to a large sheet of white construction paper. Then invite them to describe the items and pattern shown on each strip. Point out that each item represents something they might see in a parade.

2. Have children extend the pattern on each strip by using a pencil to draw additional flags, balloons, drums, or hats. Then give them crayons to incorporate colors into their patterns.

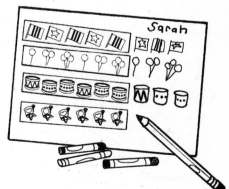

Variation: For a challenging partner activity, ask one child to begin a colored pattern, then pass it to a classmate to complete.

ABC Parade Accordion Book

Reading, Writing & Art

The linear nature of a parade makes it a perfect
subject for an alphabet parade accordion book.

1. Make 26 copies of page 52, one for each
letter of the alphabet. Assign each child a
different letter (or letters, depending on
the number of children in your group).

2. Help children cut out the pages. Then help
them brainstorm an item beginning with their letter that might appear
in a parade. For instance, *A* might be for *acrobat*, *B* for *baton twirler*, *C*
for *cymbals player*, *D* for *drum major*, and so on. Have children write
the letter and the name of their item on the banner to complete the
rhyme. Then have them draw a picture representing their rhyme. Ask
them to write their name on the line at the bottom of the page.

3. When children are finished, gather their pages and put them in
alphabetical order. Tape the pages side by side in order from left to
right. Create a reinforced front and back cover by cutting a file folder
in half. Glue each half of the folder to the back of the pages for *A* and
Z. Then fold the pages backward and forward in an accordion pattern
to complete the book.

4. Let children take turns reading the book, pulling the pages apart to
watch their parade unfold! Encourage children to name each letter and
item in their alphabet parade.

_____

is for _____

and that's what I made

to be in our alphabet parade!

A

B

C D

E

F

G

H

I

J

K

L

M

N

O

P Q

R S

T

U

V

W

X

Y

Z

Name _____

Carousel

(GREENWILLOW, 1982)

Night at the Fair

(GREENWILLOW, 1998)

Through dazzling pictures and simple text, *Carousel* recreates an exciting ride on the merry-go-round. As the book begins, the horses are still and waiting for their riders. Blurred images take children round and round, up and down, until the ride is over and the horses are still once more. *Night at the Fair* goes beyond the carousel ride, introducing children to all there is to see and do at the fair—the lights, the food, the games, and of course, more rides!

Before Reading

Before sharing *Carousel*, invite children to tell what they know about merry-go-rounds. Ask:

* Have you ever ridden on a carousel, or merry-go-round? Did you enjoy it? What did the ride feel like?

* Where can you ride on a merry-go-round? How about at an amusement park or a fair?

* How does a merry-go-round move? What kinds of animals are usually on a merry-go-round?

Before sharing *Night at the Fair*, encourage children to share any experiences they may have had at a county, state, or school fair. Ask:

* What kinds of things can you see at a fair? What kinds of activities can you do? Do you have a favorite ride to go on or a favorite game to play at the fair? What do you most like about it?

* Are there any special foods to eat at a fair? Which is your favorite?

After Reading

After reading *Carousel*, invite children to retell the sequence of the ride by asking:

* How would you describe the carousel before the ride started? Was it still or moving? What happened once the riders got on?

* How did you know when the ride was over?

(continues)

Concepts and Themes

▲ ▲ ▲ ▲ ▲ ▲

☼ carousels

☼ fairs, carnivals

☼ nighttime

Word Play

- Point out some of the unusual print features of *Carousel*. Turn to the spread about the carousel's music, and point out the large, blurry sound words. Discuss how the large words make readers think of loud sounds, and how the blurry print shows that the carousel is moving fast.

- Use *Carousel* for a mini-lesson on comparatives. Turn children's attention to the spread with the line "Fast and faster." Point out the *-er* ending and explain that this changes the word *fast* to mean *more fast*. Demonstrate the construction with the words *slow* and *slower*. Then invite children to try adding *er* to additional descriptive words, for instance, *big/bigger, small/smaller, sad/sadder,* and *happy/happier*. Be sure to point out that a *y* at the end of a word is changed to an *i* before adding *er*.

After reading *Night at the Fair*, ask:

✳ Why do you think the author said that nighttime is a great time to go to the fair? How might the fair look different during the day from the way it looks at night?

✳ How did the fair in the book compare to any fairs you have gone to? Did you recognize any of the foods, games, or rides? Which have you tried? Which did you like best and why?

Dark Nights, Bright Lights Art

As children saw in the story, nighttime is a great time to be at the fair—the bright, sparkling lights look wonderful against the black sky. Invite children to use a special art technique to recreate this effect.

1. Provide children with crayons and sheets of oaktag. Have children press hard with the crayons to completely cover their sheet with a thick layer of color. Encourage them to use a variety of bright colors, such as reds, blues, yellows, oranges, and greens. They can create any design they like, as long as the entire sheet is covered.

2. Next, have children paint over the crayon with black tempera paint and let the sheets dry overnight. When dry, give children toothpicks (orange sticks will also work well) and invite them to scratch out a nighttime fair scene. They can draw rides, signs, game booths, and so on. As children scratch out their designs, the black paint will be removed to reveal the bright colors underneath. The end result will be a dazzling night at the fair!

Five Senses Carousel Art and Writing

Going to the fair can be a festival for the senses—there is so much to see, hear, smell, taste, and touch! Let children take their senses on a ride!

1. Divide the class into small groups and provide each with two large, heavy-duty paper plates. Let children work together to paint both sides of each plate in bright, festive colors. Set aside to dry.

2. Give one copy of page 57 to each group. Help children cut out the horse patterns. Let children decorate their horses with crayons, markers, and glitter, being sure to leave the saddles blank.

3. Help children read the sentence stems on the saddles. Then talk with them about different things they might see, hear, smell, taste, and touch at a fair. For instance, they might see lights, hear music, smell popcorn, taste a pretzel, and touch a stuffed animal prize. Invite children to write words or draw a small picture on each saddle. (If desired, assign each group member a different sense.)

4. When the horses are finished and the plates are dry, help children construct their carousels:

   - Punch five evenly spaced holes around the rim of each plate.
   - Place one plate face up for the carousel bottom. Glue a drinking straw upright in each hole.
   - To make the carousel roof, turn the second plate facedown and carefully glue the tops of the straws in its holes.
   - Glue the horses to the straws, alternating their positions so that they appear to be going up and down.

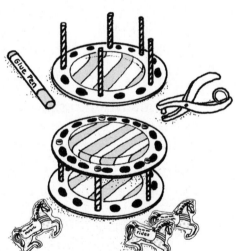

Children can turn their completed carousels by hand or place them on a turntable or Lazy Susan. Invite children to explore each group's carousel and celebrate their senses!

Book Links

The Carousel
by Liz Rosenberg
(Harcourt, 1995).

When two sisters discover
that the horses on their
park's carousel have
magically come to life, a
fantastical journey begins.

Maisy at the Fair
by Lucy Cousins
(Candlewick, 2001).

The mouse and her friends
spend a fun-filled day at
the fairgrounds, from a ride
on the carousel to the thrill
of the Ferris wheel.

Minerva Louise at the Fair
by Janet Morgan Stoeke
(Dutton, 2000).

When a chicken visits the
fairgrounds, she uses her
experiences on the farm to
misinterpret everything
she sees!

Up and Down on the
Merry-Go-Round
by Bill Martin, Jr.
& John Archambault
(Henry Holt, 1991).

Rhythmic, rhyming text
describes the sights and
sounds of a ride on the
merry-go-round from a
child's-eye view.

Classroom Fair Art & Social Studies

Why not have a fair right in the classroom? Create "tickets" from colored
construction paper, set up "game booths" around the room, award stuffed
animals or small toys as prizes, and even "sell" carnival treats! You might
even like to invite family members or another class to come to the fair.
Following are suggestions for a few simple games and foods you might try.

Carnival Games

◎ **HAVE A RING-TOSS.** Cut out the centers of paper plates to make
throwing rings. Then set a chair or stool upside-down. Have players
stand behind a masking tape line and see how many rings they can toss
onto the legs.

◎ **PLAY BEANBAG BULL'S-EYE.** Draw several concentric circles on a large
sheet of tagboard and color the center red for a bull's-eye. Place the
board on the floor and have players try to toss a beanbag to land on
the bull's-eye.

◎ **FISH FOR PRIZES!** Write prize names on construction paper fish, attach a
paper clip to each, and place in a large tub. Create a fishing pole by
tying a string to a dowel stick and tying a magnet to the end of the
string. When a player catches a fish, he or she collects the prize
indicated.

Carnival Foods

◎ **POPCORN SNACK PACKS.** Invite children to decorate small paper bags
with crayons. Pop up a batch of popcorn, pour individual servings into
the bags, and invite fairgoers to munch as they explore!

◎ **FROSTY SNOW CONES.** Put crushed ice into small plastic cups and mix
with frozen fruit juice concentrate for a fun carnival treat.

Five Senses Carousel

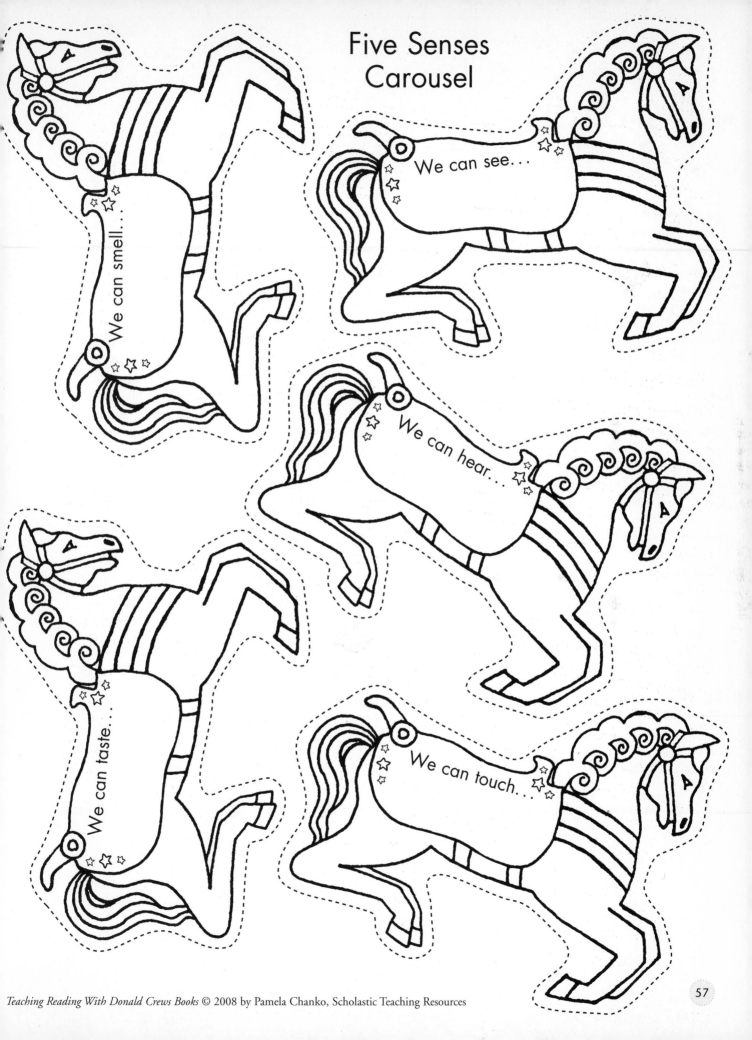

We can smell...

We can see...

We can hear...

We can taste...

We can touch...

Bigmama's

◆◆

(GREENWILLOW, 1991)

This autobiographical story recalls the author's yearly trip to his grandparents' farm, where he and his family spent each summer. The children look forward to their annual visit: when they arrive, they check to see that everything in the house and on the farm is just as it was last year—and it always is. There is a lot to see and do on the farm, from hunting for birds' nests in the barn to fishing in the pond. But perhaps the most precious summer tradition of all is the time spent with family and loved ones, creating memories to treasure forever.

Before Reading

Invite children to share their ideas about the concept of *family*. Ask:

❋ What is a family? Who are some of the people in your family?

❋ Is your family just the people who live with you, or can family members live in different places? Do you have any relatives who live far away?

❋ Have you ever gone on a special trip to see a relative or relatives? Where did you go? Did you have fun on your visit? What kinds of activities did you do with your family?

Show children the cover of the book, read the title aloud, and invite them to make predictions about the story.

❋ Where might the people on the cover be going? Who might *Bigmama* be?

After Reading

Encourage children to react and relate to the story by asking:

❋ Why do you think the children loved going to Bigmama's every year? What kinds of things did they like to do on the farm?

❋ Why do you think the children checked the house and the farm to make sure that nothing had changed since the year before? What made this place so special to them? Why did they want it to stay the same?

❋ Would you like to spend time on a farm like this one? What are some things you would do there?

✲ Do you have any special traditions you do with your family, such as a trip you take each year? What kinds of things do you do with your family on summer vacation?

You might also ask children to guess who the man at the end of the story is. Explain that he is the author of the book, all grown up. The story is about a real trip he took each summer with his family when he was a child.

Family Nicknames Chart Language Arts

In the story, the children call their grandmother "Bigmama." There are many names for grandparents (*Grandma, Abuela, Nana, Yaya*), which reflect different cultures, languages, and family traditions. Explore the cultures and traditions in your classroom with a family nickname chart.

1. Begin by writing children's names down the left side of a sheet of tagboard, leaving a fair amount of space between each. Then ask children to share what they call their grandparents. If children do not have grandparents, ask them to share a special name they have for another family member, such as a parent (*Mama, Daddy*), an aunt or uncle, or caregiver. Write any family nicknames children provide on a list next to their names in the second column of the chart. In the third column, write the family relationship (grandmother, grandfather, mother, father, and so on).

2. When the chart is complete, compare the names on children's lists:

   - Do any children have the same name for the same member of the family?
   - How do the names differ?
   - If possible, discuss the origin of each name. For instance, does the name mean "grandmother" in a different language, or is it a nickname unique to that child's particular family?
   - Do children know how the nickname got started?

Emphasize that although children may call their family members by different names, they all have one thing in common: they love each other!

Word Play

Use the story for a mini-lesson on family-member vocabulary. Page through the book, inviting children to find words that name relatives, such as *grandma, mama, sisters, brother, daddy, uncle,* and *cousins.* Write each word on the board, and then work together to brainstorm more family-member words, such as *aunt, grandfather, son, daughter, niece,* and *nephew.* You might write the words in two columns, with the male form on one side and the equivalent female relationship on the other. (For related extensions, see Family Nicknames Chart, left, and Extended Family Webs, page 60.)

Family Nicknames

	Special Name	Relationship
José	Abuela Abuelo	grandmother grandfather
Sue	Gramps Mommy	grandfather mother
Vincent	Nana Pop-Pop	grandmother father

Map the Farm   Reading: Descriptive Language

From the house to the well to the chicken coop to the barn, the descriptive detail in *Bigmama's* provides a perfect venue for mapping activities.

1. Divide the class into small groups and provide each with crayons and a large sheet of drawing paper. Encourage children to study the book's illustrations and note each place on the farm. Help them read any text that describes the location, then have each group create a map of Bigmama's farm, drawing each place and including a label.

2. When the maps are complete, display and compare children's interpretations. Groups might also act out the story in front of their maps, pointing to the location of each story event as they come to it.

Extended Family Webs   Social Studies

As children saw in the story, a family is often much more than the people you live with. Try a twist on a family tree by creating extended family webs.

1. To begin their webs, ask children to draw a large circle in the center of a large sheet of paper. Have them write the names of the family members that live with them inside the circle. (They might also draw pictures of their family members.)

2. Help children brainstorm family members that live outside their home. For each part of their extended family, have them draw a spoke from the large circle and add a smaller circle to the end of the spoke.

- If children know which members in a family unit live together (such as grandmother and grandfather or an aunt, uncle, and cousin), they can write the names of those members inside a single circle.
- Children can also write each family member's name in a separate circle.
- If children do not have extended family members, invite them to write the names of special family friends and neighbors.

Emphasize that a family can be any group of people who love and care for one another. When children's webs are complete, let each child describe his or her web. Point out that all families are different—but large or small, each is special.

Book Links

All the Places to Love
by Patricia MacLachlan
(HarperCollins, 1994).

This beautiful story tells of a boy who grows up on a farm with his parents and grandparents. From the river to the fields, each family member has a favorite place—and no matter where the boy goes, they will always be with him.

Everything Is Different at Nonna's House
by Caron Lee Cohen
(Houghton Mifflin, 2003).

When a young boy leaves his city home to visit his grandmother's farm, he discovers that the two places are very different—but that his grandmother's love is the same wherever he goes.

The Relatives Came
by Cynthia Rylant
(Simon & Schuster, 1985).

All the relatives come for their annual visit—filling the house with laughter and love all summer long.

When Lightning Comes in a Jar
by Patricia Polacco
(Philomel, 2002).

In this story, a woman recalls a glorious family reunion from her childhood. Now it is her turn to host a reunion, and to pass on each precious tradition to the new children of the family.

Shortcut

◆◆

(GREENWILLOW, 1992)

Concepts
and Themes

▲▲▲▲▲▲

☼ trains, train tracks

☼ safety

☼ following rules

In this follow-up to *Bigmama's*, Crews writes about another event from his childhood summers in Cottondale. While playing outdoors, seven children realize it is getting late and decide to take the shortcut home—by walking along the train tracks. The passenger trains run on a schedule, but a freight train might come along at any time. The suspense builds as the children hear the train's whistle and scramble to get off the tracks—just in time.

Before Reading

Begin a discussion with children about safety and following rules. Ask:

✳ Have you ever done something that a parent or caregiver told you not to do? Why weren't you supposed to do it? What happened afterwards?

✳ Why is it important to follow rules for staying safe? For instance, why should you look both ways before you cross the street?

After giving children a chance to share safety rules for a variety of situations, show the cover of the book and read the title. Ask:

✳ Why do you think the children are standing on the train tracks? Do you think this is a safe place to play? Why or why not?

✳ What is a *shortcut*? Do you know any quick ways to get from one place to another? Do you think your shortcut is safe? Why or why not?

After Reading

Invite children to retell the story and share their reactions. Ask:

✳ Why did the children stop to look and listen before taking the shortcut?

✳ Why was it dangerous for the children to walk on the tracks even though they couldn't see or hear a train when they started out?

✳ How did the children know the train was coming? How do you think they felt when they first heard the whistle?

✳ Why do you think the children decided never to take the shortcut again?

✳ What might you have done differently if you were a child in the story?

You might tell children that the story was based on something that actually happened to the author. Why do they think he wrote a book about it? Do they think the story might be a good warning for other children?

Word Play

Point out to children how the print in *Shortcut* shows action. Turn to the page where the children first hear the train, and point out the small *Whoo*. Then keep turning the pages, and ask: "What is happening to the *Whoo*?" (*It is getting bigger.*) "What do you think this means?" (*The train is getting closer, so the noise is louder.*) Then turn to the pages where the train zooms by, and point out the continuous *Klakity-Klak* that runs across the bottom of the page. Point out that this helps readers hear and see the action of the train.

Train Track Storyboard Art & Language Arts

The pattern of a train track can be used as a storyboard. Invite children to recreate the story with this unique display.

1. Provide children with a long sheet of craft paper and work with them to paint or draw a train track. Be sure to space the crossbars far apart: each square on the track will become a frame for a story scene.

2. Revisit the story with children. Help them articulate a list of story scenes, for instance: *The children listened for a train and decided to take the shortcut; The children laughed and played as they walked on the tracks; The children heard the train coming; The children ran and jumped off the tracks; The train rushed by; The children walked home on the road.*

3. Divide the class into small groups and assign each a scene to illustrate. You might create an additional group to illustrate an original story ending, showing what might have happened after the children arrived home. Have each group illustrate its scene on a frame of the train track, making sure all the frames are illustrated in sequential order. Encourage groups to write or dictate a caption for their picture.

4. When your train track storyboard is complete, display it on a classroom wall. Invite children to explore their illustrations and read the story sentences in order. Children might also enjoy acting out the story.

What Would You Do? Critical Thinking

The children in the story had an important decision to make: take the shortcut or take the road. The decision they made turned out to be a dangerous one. Help children practice smart decision-making skills with a role-playing activity.

1. Brainstorm a list of either/or situations for children to act out (you may choose to do this with the group or prepare them yourself in advance). Write each decision-making situation on a large index card. For instance: *You are playing on the sidewalk and your ball rolls into the road. Would you run after it or ask an adult for help? You are on a hike and lose your parents or caregivers. Would you run off to look for them or stay where you are?*

2. Place the index cards in a paper bag and invite partners or small groups to take turns drawing a card from the bag. Help children read and understand each situation. Then invite them to act out the decision they would make, showing what might happen next.

3. As children act out their scenes, invite the group to respond. Ask: "Do you think the role-players made the correct decision? What might happen if they had chosen differently?" As you explore each situation with the group, point out important safety issues and explain why each correct decision is the wiser one.

Stop, Look, & Listen! Social Studies

Shortcut is a story that shows just how important it is to stop, look, and listen! Invite children to create safety posters illustrating these important rules.

1. Brainstorm with children a list of safety rules that require people to stop, look, listen, or do all three. For instance, it's important to *stop* at a red light; it's important to *look* at traffic signs; it's important to *listen* during a fire drill; and it's important to do all three before crossing the street.

2. Divide the class into small groups and provide each group with markers and a sheet of posterboard. Assign each group a rule from the list and invite children to work together to design a safety poster. They might illustrate someone following the rule and write or dictate a caption.

3. Hang the posters around your classroom as a reminder for children to stay alert and stay safe!

Book Links

Country Crossing
by Jim Aylesworth
(Simon & Schuster, 1991).

On a quiet country night, a car stops at a railroad crossing just as the bell begins to ring. The passengers step out to watch the train rush by, turning the quiet evening into an exciting spectacle.

Crossing
by Philip E. Booth
(Candlewick, 2001).

A classic poem is set to beautiful paintings in this book about a rural train crossing. Children will enjoy watching safely from the sidelines as the giant train barrels past!

Curious George Takes a Train
by Margret & H. A. Rey
(Houghton Mifflin, 2002).

In another story about trains and mischief, George monkeys around with the train schedules—but redeems himself when he saves a boy from train track trouble.

Trouble on the Tracks
by Kathy Mallat
(Walker & Co., 2001).

In this suspenseful train story, the engineer hopes there will be no trouble on the tracks. The twist is that this turns out to be a boy's model train, and Trouble is his cat!

A Donald Crews Celebration: Culminating Activities

Use the following activities to wrap up your study of Donald Crews, celebrate the central themes in his work, and congratulate children on all that they've learned.

Let's Go! Art & Writing

Invite children to design and create posters advertising various modes of transportation and different destinations. Encourage them to come up with a name and slogan for their transportation company (for instance, *Tour Springfield on Bobby's Bus Line!* or *Get There Fast in Trisha's Taxi!*) Children can include posters for airlines, railroad companies, cruise ships, and so on. Invite them to illustrate their posters with pictures of the vehicle and the places it might go. For a fun extension, children can create and sell tickets and take passengers on "trips" as they fly, drive, or sail around the classroom!

Favorite Story & Vehicle Graphs Reading Response & Math

Invite children to vote for their favorite Donald Crews stories with a graph. Write the titles across a large sheet of craft paper. Then give children sheets of drawing paper and have them create an illustration to represent their favorite, for instance, a marching bandleader for *Parade*, an airplane for *Flying*, or ten black dots for *Ten Black Dots*. Have children attach their illustration beneath the appropriate title and discuss the results. You might create an additional graph of children's favorite vehicles. Do their favorite vehicles correspond with their favorite stories? Encourage children to explain their choices.

Traveling Tunes Music & Language Arts

Celebrate children's learning by inviting them to perform their own version of a favorite song. Begin by singing a few verses of the traditional version of *Old MacDonald*. Then tell children that they can turn this into a song about travel and transportation. Invite children to make up verses using their own names, a favorite vehicle, the sound it makes, and one of the vehicle's special attributes. For instance:

> Timothy, he had a train, choo-choo-choo-choo-choo.
> And on that train was a caboose, choo-choo-choo-choo-choo.
> With a choo-choo here, and a choo-choo there,
> here a choo, there a choo, everywhere a choo-choo.
> Timothy, he had a train, choo-choo-choo-choo-choo.

Stoplight Snacks Cooking

Break graham crackers into rectangular sections and let children spread peanut butter (or cream cheese) on each piece. Then have them line up a red, yellow, and green candy-coated chocolate on each cracker to create a traffic light. Now that's a treat sure to stop traffic! (Check for food allergies ahead of time.)